I0410282

THE ART of CAPTIVATING AUDIENCE

"The Unleashing Your Power through
Advanced Public Speaking Techniques"

By

Beau Parker

All Rights Reserved
©2023
Beau Parker

TABLE OF CONTENTS

Write a persuasive introduction, body, and conclusion
Use storytelling techniques to drive engagement

Chapter 3:
Regulate vocals, intonation and intonation
Breathing exercises and stress management
Reasonable use of visual aids

Chapter 4:
Analyze your audience and tailor your speech accordingly
Build relationships and maintain attention
Mix of humor and storytelling
Encourage active listening and participation

Chapter 5:

Improve your presentation skills

Create memorable anecdotes and personal stories

Manage Q&A sessions with confidence

Chapter 6:

Overcome stage fright and performance anxiety

Identify and treat the root cause of stage fright

Relaxation techniques

Exercises that involves Deep breathing

Practice visualization and active monologue

Seek support from colleagues and mentors

Gradual exposure to public speaking through practice and repetition

Conclusion

INTRODUCTION

Whether you are a student presenting, a professional speaker, or someone who just wants to improve their communication skills, this book will provide you with practical tips and strategies for becoming a presenter. proficient fake.

Overcoming the fear of public speaking is often the first and biggest hurdle for many people. We'll explore a variety of techniques to help you deal with anxiety and build the confidence to take the stage with ease.

Effective preparation is another important aspect of public speaking. This book will guide you through the process of researching your topic, organizing your thoughts, and crafting a compelling speech that will captivate your audience. Plus, we'll dive into the art of storytelling, and how to effectively use visual aids and technologies to improve your presentations.

Distribution is key when it comes to engaging our audience. In this book, we'll explore the importance of body language, voice modulation, and eye contact. You'll learn how to connect with your audience, deliver your message effectively, and leave a lasting impact.

Finally, we'll cover common challenges that can arise when speaking in public, such as handling questions, handling unexpected situations, and handling stress. By arming yourself with the skills and strategies to meet these challenges, you'll be able to confidently handle any conversation that comes your way.

Throughout this book, you'll find practical exercises, concrete examples, and helpful advice from experienced public speakers. Whether you're just starting out or looking to hone your skills, "The Art of Captivating Audience" will give you the tools and techniques to become a confident and effective communicator.

What to expect in this book

The first part of the book focuses on overcoming fear and building confidence. It explores techniques for managing anxiety, managing stress, and developing a positive mindset. The author presents various strategies and exercises that can help individuals overcome fear and boost self-confidence.

One technique discussed is the power of positive affirmations. The book explains how repeating positive statements about yourself over and over can help rewire your mind to believe in your abilities and potential. The author also emphasizes the importance of visualization and teaches readers how to successfully visualize to build confidence.

The book also delves into the concept of facing fear. He encourages readers to step out of their comfort zone and address their fears in small steps. The author offers practical advice on how to do this, such as setting achievable goals and gradually exposing yourself to scary situations.

Additionally, the book discusses the role of thinking in overcoming fear and building confidence. It explores the difference between a fixed mindset and a growth mindset, explaining how a growth mindset can lead to greater resilience and confidence. The author provides tips on how to move from a fixed mindset to a growth mindset through self-reflection and reframing negative thoughts.

Additionally, the book discusses the importance of self-care and compassion in building confidence. It highlights the need for individuals to take care of their physical and mental health, as this can have a huge impact on their confidence levels. The author provides suggestions for self-care practices and encourages readers to be kind to themselves in the process of overcoming fear and building self-confidence. Overall, the first part of the book focuses on providing practical techniques and strategies for achieving success and improving one's life. It covers topics like goal setting, visualization, positive thinking, and self-discipline. The author shares anecdotes and personal experiences to illustrate the effectiveness of these techniques.

The book emphasizes the importance of confidence and determination to succeed.

THE ART *of* CAPTIVATING AUDIENCE

UNLEASHING YOUR POWER THROUGH ADVANCED PUBLIC SPEAKING TECHNIQUES

BEAU PARKER

CHAPTER 1
UNDERSTAND THE POWER OF PUBLIC SPEAKING

Effective communication is essential in almost every aspect of our lives. Here are some reasons why this is important:

1. Relationship Building: Effective communication helps build and maintain positive relationships with others. It allows for clear understanding and empathy, which in turn promotes trust and cooperation.

2. Encourage productivity: Good communication within organizations and teams leads to higher productivity. When everyone is on the same page and understands their roles and

expectations, tasks can be completed more efficiently.

3. Conflict resolution: Miscommunication is often the root of conflict. By communicating effectively, conflicts can be resolved and resolved, leading to healthier and more harmonious relationships.

4. Sharing of ideas and information: Communication enables the sharing of ideas, knowledge and information. Successful organizations encourage open communication, enabling innovation, creativity, and continuous learning.

5. Make informed decisions: Effective communication ensures that all relevant information is conveyed correctly, helping individuals and

organizations make informed decisions. It enables the exchange of views, facilitating better decision-making and problem-solving processes.

6. Enhance personal development: Good communication skills are indispensable for personal growth and development. The ability to speak clearly and to listen actively improves self-awareness, communication skills, and emotional intelligence.

7. Avoid misunderstandings: Effective communication helps to avoid misunderstandings and misunderstandings. By clearly communicating thoughts and intentions, misunderstandings and misinterpretations can be minimized,

conflict is reduced, and understanding is fostered.

8. Support diverse and inclusive environments: In a diverse and inclusive environment, all individuals are treated with respect, dignity and fairness, regardless of race, ethnicity, gender, or gender. their gender, sexual orientation, age, religion, disability or any other characteristic. This not only benefits the individuals themselves, but also contributes to a more productive and creative working environment.

Benefits of becoming a fluent public speaker:

There are numerous benefits to becoming a fluent public speaker.

These are some of the important advantages:

1. Improved communication skills: Public speaking requires you to articulate your thoughts clearly and concisely. As you hone your public speaking skills, your overall communication skills, including listening and responding, will naturally improve.

2. Enhanced self-confidence: Being able to speak confidently and deliver your message effectively in front of an audience boosts your self-confidence. Over time, you'll become more comfortable expressing your ideas and engaging with others, both in formal presentations and everyday conversations.

3. Better persuasion and influence: Fluent public speakers have the power to persuade and influence others. By mastering the art of delivering compelling speeches, you can sway opinions, inspire action, and make a lasting impact on your audience.

4. Increased professional opportunities: Effective public speaking is highly valued in various professional fields. By becoming a fluent public speaker, you open doors to career advancement, leadership positions, and networking opportunities. You'll be able to showcase your expertise, share your ideas, and leave a lasting impression on employers, clients, and colleagues.

5. Improved critical thinking and problem-solving skills: Preparing and

delivering public speeches requires thorough research, analysis, and organization of ideas. This process enhances your critical thinking and problem-solving abilities, enabling you to approach complex issues with clarity and coherence.

6. Heightened ability to handle and overcome fear: Fear of public speaking is one of the most common fears for many people. By becoming a fluent public speaker, you not only improve your communication skills, but you also develop a heightened ability to handle and overcome fear.

Public speaking requires you to face your fear head-on and step out of your comfort zone. As you repeatedly expose yourself to public speaking situations, you become more comfortable and confident in your abilities.

Overcoming fear and building confidence:
Overcoming fear and building confidence can be challenging, but it is possible with consistent effort and a positive mindset. Here are some tips to help you overcome fear and build confidence:

1.   Identify your fears: Start by identifying the specific fears that are holding you back. Write them down and reflect on why they make you afraid.

2.   Face your fears slowly : Begin with taking small steps towards facing your fears. Break them down into

manageable tasks and gradually expose yourself to them. This process is known as "exposure therapy" and helps desensitize you to your fears over time.

3. Fight against negative thoughts: Fear usually stems from negative thoughts and self-doubt. Fight these negative thoughts by replacing them with positive and realistic ones. Remind yourself of your strengths, past successes, and the possibilities for growth.

4. Seek support: Share your fears and insecurities with trusted friends, family, or a therapist. They can offer guidance, encouragement, and different perspectives that may help you overcome your fears.

5. Celebrate small victories: Acknowledge and celebrate the small victories along the way. Every step you take towards facing your fears and building confidence is worth celebrating. This positive reinforcement will help motivate you to keep going.

6. Practice self-care: Taking care of yourself physically, mentally, and emotionally is crucial for building confidence. Engage in activities that make you feel good, such as exercise, hobbies, meditation, or spending time with loved ones.

7. Embrace failure as a learning opportunity: A learning opportunity refers to any situation or experience that enables individuals to acquire new knowledge, develop skills or gain

insights. It can be formal, such as attending a lecture, workshop, or class, or informal, like watching a documentary or reading a book.

CHAPTER 2
MASTER THE BASICS OF SPEECH PREPARATION

When it comes to choosing the right topic for your audience, there are several key factors to consider. By understanding your audience's interests, needs, and preferences, you can choose a topic that works for them and effectively engages them.

These are some tips that will help you make the right decision:

1. Research your audience: Take the time to gather information about your audience's demographics, interests, and preferences. This can be done through surveys, data analysis, or even casual conversations with a sample group. Understanding their

background will help you tailor your theme to their specific needs and desires.

2. Hot Topic Analysis: Stay up to date with current events, industry trends, and social media discussions. Analyzing attention-grabbing topics can provide valuable insights into what your audience might be interested in. Choosing an existing topic that is relevant and resonates with your audience can increase your chances of capturing their attention.

3. Consider their level of knowledge: Assess how familiar your audience is with the topic you are considering. Are they a beginner or an expert in the field? Avoid topics that are too basic or too advanced for your audience. Instead, aim for a topic that is within

their reach, but also gives them something new and valuable.

4. Solve their pain points: Identify the challenges or problems your audience is facing and choose a topic that offers practical solutions or valuable insights. By addressing their pain points, you demonstrate that you understand their needs and are committed to helping them overcome challenges.

Conduct extensive research and gather reliable sources:
Mastering the art of Captivating Audience is a skill that can dramatically improve our personal and professional lives. Whether presenting a proposal to a colleague, speaking at a conference, or simply engaging in effective communication with others,

the ability to speak confidently and eloquently in public is valued. High. . However, acquiring this skill requires more than just natural talent; it requires conducting extensive research and gathering reliable sources.

The first step to conducting thorough research into the art of public speaking is to identify specific areas where you want to improve. Speaking confidently in front of a large audience may be the main focus, while others may want pronunciation, body language, or persuasion techniques. Clearly identifying specific areas for improvement will allow for more targeted research. Once the areas for improvement have been identified, it is essential to gather reliable sources. Credible sources give credibility and value to the research conducted, ensuring that the knowledge gained is accurate and applicable in real-life situations. Credible sources can come in a variety of forms, including books, scientific articles, reputable websites, interviews with experts, and online materials from reputable academic institutions.

Books and scientific articles provide in-depth knowledge of the subject, often presenting theory, case studies, and practical advice. Studying well-known authors who specialize in public speaking, such as Dale Carnegie or Nancy Duarte, can provide a great platform to learn and hone your skills. Additionally, scientific articles can be found in academic journals that provide evidence-based research. These articles are written by experts in the field and often go through a rigorous peer-review process to ensure accuracy and quality. They can provide insight into the psychological and communicative aspects of public speaking, as well as explore the latest trends and developments in the field.

Write a persuasive introduction, body, and conclusion:
 Writing a compelling introduction, body, and conclusion is essential to any piece of writing, as it helps engage the reader, present the argument or information effectively, and leaves a lasting impact. . Whether you are writing an essay, an article or even a speech, these three factors play an important role in ensuring the success of your writing.

Above all, a compelling introduction will grab the reader's attention and set the tone for the rest of the paper. It should introduce the topic, provide background information, and present a clear thesis or main argument. An effective introduction can include a stimulating question, an interesting anecdote, or a shocking statistic. By capturing the reader's interest, you create a solid foundation for the rest of the article.

The body of your work is where you develop and present your ideas or arguments in a logical and coherent manner. Each paragraph should focus on a main or minor point and provide supporting evidence or examples to support your point. The key is to organize your thoughts in a structured way, use topic sentences to introduce each paragraph, and move smoothly between ideas. By presenting clear and well-grounded arguments, you can convince your readers and keep them engaged throughout your writing. It is important to avoid introducing new information in the conclusion, but to restate your main points and potentially offer a new point of view or call to action.

Use storytelling techniques to drive engagement:
Storytelling is a powerful tool that can engage and engage an audience. Here are some techniques for using storytelling to drive engagement:

1. Start with a compelling story: Start your story with a compelling opening line, compelling question, or

thrilling event to instantly capture your audience's attention.

2. Develop personalities you can relate to: Create personalities your audience can connect with emotionally. Make them lovable, flawed, and relatable so your audience feels invested in their journey.

3. Create suspense and tension: Incorporate elements of suspense and tension to engage your audience. Use controversies, unexpected twists, or unresolved conflicts to keep them guessing and eager to know what will happen next.

4. Use vivid descriptions: Paint a vivid picture with your words to bring the listener into the story. Use sensory

details to help them visualize the scene and feel immersed in the story.

5. Show, don't tell: Instead of explaining things in person, show your audience through action, dialogue, and vivid descriptions. Let them draw conclusions and create their own mental picture of the story.

6. Incorporating emotions: Capturing your audience's emotions by creating moments of joy, surprise, sadness, or fear. By engaging their emotions, you can make them more invested in the story and its outcome.

7. Use dialogue: Dialogue adds life and authenticity to a story. Create compelling and realistic dialogue between characters to reveal their

personalities, intentions, and contradictions.

CHAPTER 3
DEVELOP ENGAGING DELIVERY SKILLS

Regulate vocals, intonation and intonation:
These are important aspects of speech that can enhance communication and make the speaker's message - Nonverbal communication: body language, gestures and eye contact more engaging and impactful .

Speech modulation refers to changing the pitch, volume, and rhythm of speech. It involves the use of different tones and inflections to convey emotions, emphasize certain words or phrases, and capture the listener's attention. By varying pitch and volume, speakers can create dynamic and engaging transmissions that add depth to their message.

On the other hand, intonation refers to the rise and fall of pitch patterns in a phrase or sentence. It helps to convey meaning, mood and attitude. For example, increased intonation at the end of a sentence could indicate a question, while decreased intonation could mean a statement or a conclusion. Intonation patterns also play an important role in expressing emotion and conveying emphasis.

Slideshow refers to the act of making one's voice loud and clear enough to reach and engage the intended audience, whether a small group or a large crowd. Good projection ensures that all viewers can hear and understand the speaker, even when speaking in a larger room or using a microphone. It involves using the diaphragm and controlling breathing to create a powerful, resonant voice.

When used together effectively, voice modulation, intonation, and pronunciation can greatly improve a speaker's ability to communicate and connect with their audience. They allow speakers to convey emotion, engage their listeners, emphasize key points, and maintain interest throughout their presentation.

Non-verbal communication: body language, gestures and eye contact: Nonverbal communication plays an important role in effective public speaking. In fact, studies show it makes up a significant percentage of overall communication. It includes body language, gestures, and eye contact that, when mastered, can greatly enhance the conveyance and impact of a speaker's message.

Body language is how we use our bodies to convey messages and emotions. Paying attention to body language helps the speaker maintain an open and confident posture, thereby establishing a positive connection with the audience. Good posture, such as upright posture, creates a sense of competence and confidence. Conversely, slouching or fidgeting gait can make the speaker appear nervous or disinterested. By consciously adjusting body language, speakers can create an environment that fosters engagement and trust.

Gestures are nonverbal actions that complement and reinforce the speaker's message. Using appropriate gestures can help clarify ideas, emphasize key points, and add visual interest to speech. For example, pointing at an object, using hand gestures to indicate size or direction, or even applying expressions appropriate to what is being discussed can help an audience understand and retain information. However, excessive or irrelevant gestures can be awkward and should be avoided. Eye contact is crucial to fostering a connection with your audience. Maintaining steady, intentional eye contact throughout speech conveys trust, credibility, and sincerity. This creates a sense of inclusion, helping the audience feel recognized and engaged. However, it is essential to find a balance. While maintaining regular eye contact is important, constant staring can be frustrating for the audience. It's important to make eye contact with different people in the crowd, making sure everyone feels included. It shows that you really care about connecting with each person and their reactions.

Breathing exercises and stress management:
Breathing exercises and stress management can be very effective in reducing stress, promoting relaxation, and improving overall health. Here are some techniques that can help you:

1. Deep breathing: Sit or lie comfortably and breathe slowly and

deeply. Inhale through your nose, fill your stomach with air, and slowly exhale through your mouth. Focus on your breath and release any tension or tension with each exhale.

2. Box breath: Breathe in deeply for a count of 4, hold your breath for a count of 4, exhale slowly for a count of 4, then hold your breath again for a count of 4 before repeating. Visualize yourself drawing a box with your breath at each step.

3. Breathe 4-7-8: Inhale through your nose for a count of 4, hold your breath for a count of 7, and exhale through your mouth for a count of 8. This exercise can help reduce anxiety and create a sense of relaxation.

4. Conscious Breathing: Close your eyes and pay attention to your breathing. Observe each inhale and exhale without trying to control or modify it. Let thoughts or distractions come and go without judgment, and just focus on your breath.

5. Progressive muscle relaxation: Start by contracting the muscles in your toes, then work your way through different muscle groups in your body. Hold the stretch for a few seconds and then release, allowing the muscles to relax completely. Repeat this process for each muscle group, including legs, abs, chest, arms, and shoulders. This technique helps relieve muscle tension and promotes overall relaxation.

6. Deep breathing: Breathe slowly and deeply, inhaling through your nose and exhaling through your mouth. Breathing deeply is a relaxation technique that can help reduce stress and promote feelings of calm.

Reasonable use of visual aids:
Proper use of visual aids is an important skill to have in a variety of professional environments, such as classrooms, conference rooms, and conference presentations. Here are some tips for using visual aids effectively:

1. Choose the right visual aids: Choose the right visual aids for your content and purpose. Options can include PowerPoint slides, tables, charts, diagrams, videos, and props.

Make sure the visual aids are relevant and support your message.

2. Keep it simple: Avoid cluttering your visual aids with too much information. Use concise text, clear images, and clean design. Simplify complex ideas into easy-to-understand visuals.

3. Use the right font size and color: Use an easy-to-read font and make sure the text is easily readable from a distance. Choose high-contrast colors to improve readability. Avoid using too many colors or fonts that can distract the audience.

4. Stay consistent: Use a consistent layout, color scheme, and font style across all of your visual media. This helps create a professional,

cohesive look and avoids visual distractions.

5. Use visual aids as an addition, not a replacement: Visual aids enhance your presentation, not replace your speech. Use them to highlight key points, illustrate concepts, or provide examples.

6. Practice with visual aids: Get familiar with visual aids and practice using them in your presentations. This will help you feel more confident and comfortable during the actual presentation.

7. The Right Time for Your Visual Media: Introduce and display visual aids at the right times in your presentation to improve understanding and engagement. It is

important to time the introduction and render correctly to maintain a smooth flow and maximize impact. Here are some tips on how to do it:

CHAPTER 4
CONNECT WITH YOUR AUDIENCE

Analyze your audience and tailor your speech accordingly:

When preparing a speech, it is essential to analyze your audience and tailor your message accordingly. This helps ensure that your pitch resonates with your audience, keeps them interested, and delivers your message effectively. Here are some steps you can take to analyze your audience and tailor your speech to their needs:

1. Research your audience: Gather information about your audience's demographics, interests, knowledge levels, and perspectives. This can be done through surveys, interviews or simply by observing their characteristics. Understand their age,

gender, education level, cultural background, and any other relevant information.

2. Define their needs and expectations: Determine what your audience wants from your speech and what they want to gain from it. Consider their concerns, concerns, and major challenges they may face. Meeting these needs will help you establish credibility and connect with your audience.

3. Adjust language and tone: Adjust your language and vocabulary so that your listeners can understand. Also, consider the right tone for your speech based on your audience's preferences. It can range from formal to casual, depending on the setting and context.

4. Personalize examples and references: Use examples, stories, and references that are familiar and relevant to your audience. This helps them understand your message and creates a sense of inclusion. Consider using local or personal anecdotes that they can easily understand and appreciate.

5. Express your message appropriately: Depending on your audience and purpose, expressing your message appropriately is essential for effective communication.

Build relationships and maintain attention:
Relationship building is key to building a positive relationship with someone and getting their attention.

Here are some key strategies to achieve this:

1. Active listening: Give your full attention to the person you're interacting with by maintaining eye contact, nodding, and responding appropriately.

2. Use positive body language: smile, maintain an open posture, and use appropriate facial expressions to show that you are engaged and genuinely interested in the conversation.

3. Ask some open-ended questions: Encourage the person to share more about their thoughts, opinions, or experiences. Not only will this keep them engaged, but it will also show that you appreciate their contribution.

4. Find common ground: Look for shared interests, experiences, or beliefs that can create a sense of connection. This can help build rapport and make the conversation more enjoyable for both parties.

5. Show empathy and understanding: Acknowledge the person's feelings and try to understand their point of view. This helps create an environment that is supportive and promotes mutual trust and respect.

6. Personalize the conversation: Use the person's name, refer to previous conversations or shared experiences, and show that you remember them in detail. It shows that you value them as an individual.

7. Use the right humor: Using humor in conversation can help keep things light and pleasant, but be mindful of the person's preferences and circumstances to avoid offending or alienating Surname.

8. Sincerity and Sincerity: People can often sense when someone is dishonest or fake. People value authenticity and are more likely to trust and connect with you when they feel you are authentic.

Mix of humor and storytelling: Presentations or speeches can be a very effective way to engage your audience and make your message more memorable. Here are some tips for incorporating humor and storytelling into your presentations:

1. Know your audience: Before combining humor and storytelling, it is essential to understand your audience and their interests. Different types of humor work for different people, so try to tailor it to their taste.

2. Start with a story: Start your presentation with a compelling and relevant story. It could be a personal anecdote, an inspirational story, or even a fictional account that supports your message.

3. Use humor strategically: Humor can break the ice, reduce stress, and make your presentations more interesting. Incorporate funny jokes, puns, or anecdotes to create laughter and create a positive environment. However, make sure that your humor

is relevant to the topic and doesn't offend anyone.

4. Make it easy to understand: Bringing relevant experiences or situations into your presentation will help your audience connect with your message. Relativity increases engagement and makes your content more memorable.

5. Concise: Be mindful of the length of the story and the level of humor you include. It's important to strike a balance so your presentation doesn't lose focus or become too long.

6. Use visuals: Visual aids, such as images or videos, can enhance your storytelling and bring humor to your presentation. Consider incorporating fun images or short video clips that fit

your story and add an element of humor. For example, if you're telling a funny story about an incident at work, you could include a relevant humorous meme or a clip from a comedy show that illustrates the situation.

Encourage active listening and participation:
1. Set clear expectations: Clearly communicate to everyone involved the importance of active listening and participation. Let them know that their input is appreciated and encourage them to participate actively in the discussion.

2. Create a safe and open environment: Cultivate an atmosphere where

individuals feel comfortable expressing their thoughts and opinions. Encourage respectful and constructive dialogue and openness to different points of view.

3. Create opportunities to participate: Make sure everyone has the opportunity to share their ideas, thoughts, and questions. Encourage individuals to contribute in meetings, training sessions, or group activities. Provide opportunities for small group discussions or brainstorming sessions to ensure active participation.

5. Use active listening strategies: Model active listening behaviors, such as maintaining eye contact, nodding, and paraphrasing what others have said. Encourage participants to ask clarifying questions and actively

participate in the conversation by sharing their thoughts and opinions based on what they have heard.

6. Pause and Reflect: Give participants regular time to pause and reflect on what has been said. Give them time to think and respond. This can be especially helpful for calmer people, who may need more time to process information and contribute.

7. Incentive: Offer incentives or rewards for active participation. This can be as simple as recognizing valuable contributions or more formal rewards such as certificates or small gifts. However, keep in mind that incentives should not overwhelm the importance of real participation and active listening.

8. Use supportive tools and techniques: Use tools and techniques that encourage active listening.

CHAPTER 5
IMPROVE YOUR PRESENTATION SKILLS

Use effective slide and graphic design:
Can greatly enhance the impact and communication value of a presentation. Here are some tips for using graphics and slide design effectively:

1. Keep it simple: Avoid cluttering your slides with too much text or graphics. Stick to a clean, minimalist design that helps the main message stand out.

2. Use high-quality images: Choose clear, relevant, high-resolution images.

3. Use consistent fonts and colors: Choose a color scheme and font style that matches your brand or theme and use them consistently throughout your slides. This helps create a cohesive and visually appealing presentation.

4. Use visual hierarchy: Organize your content in a logical and visually appealing way using visual hierarchy. This means using different font sizes, colors, and styles to emphasize important points and create a clear flow of information.

5. Use tables and graphs: Visualize your data using tables and graphs instead of presenting numbers or raw text. This makes complex information easier to understand and more visually appealing.

6. Limit the use of animations: While animations can be useful for highlighting key points, too many animations or overly complicated transitions can be distracting. Use animation sparingly and focus on the content and message you are trying to convey.

7. Readable design: Make sure your text is legible by using font sizes and types that are appropriate for your screen size and audience. Avoid using overly decorative or difficult-to-read fonts as they can make the text harder to understand. Use clear, easy-to-read fonts, such as Arial, Helvetica, or Times New Roman.

Integrating multimedia tools and technologies:
- Enhance the learning experience by integrating multimedia tools and technologies into the classroom

1. Improve engagement: Multimedia tools and technologies can capture students' attention and make the learning process more engaging. Videos, interactive presentations, and animations can effectively communicate complex concepts and stimulate students' curiosity.

2. Personalized Learning: Multimedia tools allow for a personalized learning experience because they allow students to interact with content at the speed and format of their choice. For example, students can access online resources, such as

educational videos and interactive exercises, tailored to their individual needs.

3. Simulation and virtual reality: Multimedia tools can provide realistic simulations and virtual reality experiences that allow students to learn through hands-on and immersive activities. For example, students can virtually explore historic sites, perform science experiments, or practice real-world skills in a controlled environment.

4. Collaborative learning: Multimedia tools facilitate collaboration between students. With the help of technology, students can work together on projects, online discussions or virtual classrooms in real time. This promotes teamwork, communication

skills and the exchange of ideas among colleagues.

5. Access to a wide range of information: Multimedia tools allow students to access a wide variety of information. Online databases, e-books, and multimedia platforms provide a variety of resources that can be used to supplement classroom instruction and support independent study.

6. Creative assessment methods: Technology can enable teachers to use innovative assessment methods. For example, online quizzes, multimedia presentations, and digital portfolios can provide a more complete picture of student learning and progress. These assessment methods allow for more customization and flexibility, as

well as the ability to integrate different types of media and resources. For example, online quizzes can be used to test students' knowledge and understanding of specific topics or concepts.

Create memorable anecdotes and personal stories:
Creating memorable anecdotes and personal stories is an art form that requires creativity and careful thought. Here are some tips to help you create compelling and memorable stories:

1. Start with a catchy hook: Start your anecdote or story with a compelling opening line or sentence that grabs your listener's attention and makes them want to know more.

2. Use vivid language and sexy details: Smoothly combine descriptive language and sexy details to paint a vivid picture in the viewer's mind. It will make your story more engaging and memorable.

3. Focus on the central theme or message: Decide on the main message or theme you want to convey through your story. This will help you structure your story around a central idea and make it easier for your audience to understand and remember.

4. Show, don't tell: Instead of just stating facts or events, try to show your audience what happened using dialogue, action, and emotion. This will make your story more dynamic and engaging.

5. Inject humor or emotion: Adding humor or emotion to your anecdotes and stories can make them more interesting and relevant. Finding the right balance between emotion or humor will keep your audience engaged and improve their memory of your story.

6. Keep it brief: While providing enough detail is key to making your story interesting, try to avoid unnecessary or excessive details that can detract from the impact. its motion. Keep the story focused, short, and to the point.

7. Incorporate personal experiences: Sharing your own personal experiences can help make your writing more relevant and engaging. For example, if you write a

convincing essay about the importance of recycling, you could share a personal story about how you have witnessed the harmful effects of garbage while hiking.

Manage Q&A sessions with confidence:
Requires preparation, clear communication, and a calm demeanor. Here are some tips to help you handle Q&A sessions with confidence:

1. Be prepared: Anticipate possible questions and prepare answers in advance. Research the topic thoroughly and gather as much information as possible. This will help you feel more confident and informed during the session.

2. Active listening: Listen attentively to the questions posed by the audience and make sure you fully understand before answering. Take a moment to pause and think about the question if necessary, to avoid rushing into an answer.

3. Stay calm and composed: It's natural to feel a little nervous during a Q&A session. Take a deep breath and remind yourself that you understand the subject well. Maintain a calm and confident demeanor, which will also help the audience feel at ease.

4. Pause before answering: Take a moment to organize your thoughts before answering a question. This will help you formulate a clear and concise answer. You might say, That's a

good question, let me think about it for a moment.

5. Honesty and transparency: If you don't know the answer to a question, admit it. Being honest is better than providing incorrect information. Offer to find the answer and contact the person later.

6. Provide concise and clear answers: Keep your answers short and precise. Avoid wandering or deviating. Use simple language and avoid argon or technical jargon that the person may not understand. Focus on answering the question asked to provide a clear and direct answer.

CHAPTER 6
OVERCOME STAGE FRIGHT AND PERFORMANCE ANXIETY

Identify and treat the root cause of stage fright:
Stage fright can be a debilitating experience that prevents individuals from fully expressing themselves and realizing their full potential. Identifying and addressing the root causes of stage fright is key to overcoming this challenge. Here are some tips that will help you:

1. Introspection and Awareness: Take time to reflect on your stage fright and try to identify the triggers or specific situations that cause it. Is it the fear of being judged or making a mistake? Understanding the

underlying cause will help you treat it more effectively.

2. Preparation and practice: One of the main causes of stage fright is lack of confidence in one's own abilities. By thoroughly rehearsing and preparing for your performance, you can build a strong foundation of skills and knowledge, which can give you a lot more confidence on stage.

3. Positive self-talk and visualization: Replace negative thoughts and self-doubt with positive affirmations. Visualize yourself performing confidently and successfully on stage. This technique can help reframe your thinking and reduce anxiety.

4. Breathing and relaxation techniques: Deep breathing exercises and

progressive muscle relaxation techniques can help calm your nerves and reduce the physical symptoms of stage fright. Regular practice of these techniques before performing will help your body relax in stressful situations.

5. Exposure therapy: Gradually expose yourself to performing in front of others to make yourself less sensitive to fear. Start with a small supportive audience and work your way up to a larger, more important audience. This gradual exposure can help build confidence and reduce stage fright over time.

6. Use relaxation techniques and deep breathing exercises:
These things can help overcome anxiety and improve speaking skills

significantly. Here's a note on how to use these techniques effectively:

Dear President,

Public speaking can be both exciting and challenging. It's completely normal to feel nervous and nervous before giving a speech or presentation. However, by incorporating relaxation techniques and deep breathing exercises into your routine, you can learn the skills you need to become a fluent and confident public speaker.

Relaxation techniques:
1. Incremental muscle relaxation: This technique involves tensing and then relaxing each muscle group in your body, starting at your toes and

working your way up. It helps to release stress and reduce anxiety.

2. Visualize: Before your speech, imagine yourself presenting confidently and receiving a positive response from the audience. Visualization techniques can help reduce stress and build confidence.

3. Mindfulness meditation: Practicing mindfulness meditation allows you to focus on the present moment, thereby reducing anxiety. Spend a few minutes a day on this exercise to increase your ability to focus during speeches.

Exercises that involves Deep breathing:
1. Diaphragm breathing: Place one hand on the diaphragm, just below

the ribcage, and inhale slowly and deeply. This exercise slows your heart rate and promotes relaxation, allowing you to speak more calmly and clearly.

2. Quadruple breathing: Inhale deeply for four seconds, hold your breath for four seconds, exhale for four seconds, then hold your breath for four seconds before repeating the cycle. This technique helps you to slow down your breathing and bring more oxygen to your body, which helps to relax and reduce stress. It can be done anywhere and at any time, making it a useful tool for everyday stress management.

Practice visualization and active monologue:

There are two powerful tools that can greatly impact your mindset and help you achieve your goals. Here are some tips for incorporating these practices into your daily routine:

1. Find a quiet, comfortable place: Start by finding a quiet, peaceful place where you won't be disturbed. This will allow you to focus fully on visualization and positive self-talk.

2. Set goals: Before you start practicing, set clear goals for what you want to achieve. Whether it's achieving a specific goal, improving self-confidence, or reducing stress, be clear about what you want to envision and promote through positive self-talk.

3. Visualization: Close your eyes and create a vivid mental image of you achieving the desired outcome. Use all your senses to make the visualization as detailed and realistic as possible. Imagine what you will feel, what you will see and the energy surrounding your success.

4. Positive self-talk: Replace negative self-talk with positive, uplifting statements. Be your own cheerleader and repeat affirmations that build your ability and strength. For example, instead of saying I can't do this, say I am capable, I have the skills and determination to succeed.

5. Use the present tense: When practicing positive self-talk, use sentences in the present tense to reaffirm your confidence. Say things

like "I am confident", "I am worthy", and "I am capable". It helps change your thinking and reinforces positive thoughts in the present moment.

Seek support from colleagues and mentors:
It is not an easy task and often requires constant effort, practice, and guidance. Seeking the support of colleagues and mentors can play an important role in honing this skill and becoming a confident and effective public speaker.

Colleagues can provide a valuable source of support when it comes to mastering public speaking. They can provide a safe, non-judgmental space to practice and get feedback. By joining public speaking clubs or joining public speaking groups, individuals can connect with like-minded people who are also on their way to improving their public speaking skills. they. Participating in group meetings where participants take turns speaking and offering constructive criticism can greatly improve their speaking skills. Additionally, attending other people's presentations and learning from their strengths and weaknesses can broaden one's perspective and promote personal growth as a speaker.

On the other hand, a mentor can offer personalized advice and expertise. They are experienced people who have mastered the art of public speaking and can offer useful ideas and techniques. Mentors can provide direct feedback, identify areas for improvement, and suggest specific strategies to overcome weaknesses. Their advice can be tailored to each individual's unique needs and goals, providing a clear path of growth. In addition, mentors can share personal anecdotes, tips, and tricks that have helped them on their journey to public speaking, inspiring and motivating individuals to push boundaries and reach their full potential.

Gradual exposure to public speaking through practice and repetition:
Like any skill, it can be improved and mastered with gradual exposure and consistent practice. The key to becoming a fluent public speaker is repetition, familiarizing yourself

with the content, and practicing different techniques.

Gradual exposure to public speaking is crucial to overcoming the initial fear and anxiety associated with it. Start by speaking in front of a small, friendly audience, such as family or close friends. It helps build confidence and comfort when sharing thoughts and ideas in public. As trust grows, it is important to expand exposure to a wider audience. Joining public speaking clubs or participating in public speaking events can provide valuable opportunities to confront and overcome any lingering fears. Accepting invitations to speak at events, conferences, or even in professional or academic settings gradually expands the comfort zone and allows for continuous improvement.

Practice and repetition are the keys to mastering the art of public fluency. When overcoming fear, it is important to focus on content and delivery. Start by thoroughly researching and understanding the topic presented. This not only helps build confidence but also enhances the speaker's knowledge and credibility.

Repeat the speech several times, both silently and loudly. Practice in front of a mirror to observe facial expressions, posture, and gestures. This allows for self-assessment and helps identify areas for improvement. Recording and reviewing rehearsals can provide valuable information and provide an opportunity for self-criticism.

Also, consider getting feedback from others by having a trusted friend or family member listen to your speech and offer constructive criticism. They can notice things you've missed and offer suggestions for improvement.

Another useful practice is to simulate a real speech environment.

CONCLUSIONS

The Art of Captivating Audience is an exceptional resource for anyone looking to improve their communication skills and become an effective public speaker. The book offers comprehensive instructions, practical techniques and valuable advice applicable to beginners as well as experienced.

One of the main strengths of this book is the emphasis on developing public fluency. The author, with his rich experience in this field, explains the importance of mastering the linguistic and non-verbal aspects of communication. By offering a variety of exercises and strategies to improve pronunciation, body language, and confidence, the book provides readers with the tools they need to speak in front of a large audience.

Plus, the author's approachable writing style and engaging anecdotes make the book easy to understand and enjoyable to read. Concepts are presented in a logical and structured manner, allowing the reader to gradually grasp the material and apply it at their own pace. With each chapter building on the knowledge gained from the previous one, the book ensures a smooth learning experience for the reader.

Another notable aspect of this book is its suitability for different speaking occasions. Whether it is a business presentation, public lecture or social gathering, the principles and strategies provided in the book can be adapted to suit different contexts and audiences. different. In addition, the inclusion of real-life examples and case studies not only demonstrates the effectiveness of the techniques, but also illustrates the persuasive power of public speaking. Overall, "The Art of Captivating Audience" is a valuable resource for anyone looking to improve their public speaking skills. The book provides a comprehensive guide to all aspects of public speaking, from managing anxiety to structuring a persuasive speech.

www.ingramcontent.com/pod-product-compliance
Lightning Source LLC
Chambersburg PA
CBHW062234290526
45794CB00006B/2286